A Creative Festival

Edited By Lynsey Evans

First published in Great Britain in 2024 by:

Young Writers
Remus House
Coltsfoot Drive
Peterborough
PE2 9BF
Telephone: 01733 890066
Website: www.youngwriters.co.uk

FOREWORD

Welcome Reader, to a world of dreams.

For Young Writers' latest competition, we asked our writers to dig deep into their imagination and create a poem that paints a picture of what they dream of, whether it's a make-believe world full of wonder or their aspirations for the future.

The result is this collection of fantastic poetic verse that covers a whole host of different topics. Let your mind fly away with the fairies to explore the sweet joy of candy lands, join in with a game of fantasy football, or you may even catch a glimpse of a unicorn or another mythical creature. Beware though, because even dreamland has dark corners, so you may turn a page and walk into a nightmare!

Whereas the majority of our writers chose to stick to a free verse style, others gave themselves the challenge of other techniques such as acrostics and rhyming couplets. We also gave the writers the option to compose their ideas in a story, so watch out for those narrative pieces too!

Each piece in this collection shows the writers' dedication and imagination – we truly believe that seeing their work in print gives them a well-deserved boost of pride, and inspires them to keep writing, so we hope to see more of their work in the future!

CONTENTS

Clement Bulmer (8) 64
Summer Greenland (8) 65
Ameen Yaqoob (8) 66
Vincent Wang (8) 67
Amelia Sethi (8) 68
Hadi Tabib (8) 69
Cooper Campbell (8) 70
Yunuo (George) Song (8) 71
Hedda Husvaeg Derome (8) 72
Nico Turney (7) 73
Theo Asghar (7) 74

Holy Ghost Catholic Primary School, Wandsworth

Emma Marie Scicchitano (8) 75
Izzy Pass (11) 76
Arun Agostinelli (9) 78
Giulia Galtieri (10) 80
Hugo Herburt-Burns (9) 82
Kyla Agostinelli (7) 84
Alex Catalogna (8) 86
Maeva Moore (8) 88
Eibhlin Reynolds Paul (9) 89
Millie Wittet (10) 90
Eva Molloy (8) 91
Harry Young (7) 92
Olann Pearce (9) 93
Daniel Kaiza (9) 94
Mariana Stephenson (8) 95
Isabella Diana (9) 96
Elizabeth Wells (10) 97
Amelia Jackson-Dauncey (10) 98
Richard Matuszewski (9) 99
Eva Wittet (10) 100
Giorgio Gambacorta (9) 101
Garance Roch (9) 102
Aliénor Demortreux (9) 103
Joella-Eden Asamoah (11) 104
Angelica Adami (9) 105
Haizea Waterworth (8) 106
Etienne Conti (8) 107
Dylan Medeiros (10) 108
Danny Slater (7) 109

Sofia Fattouche (7) 110
Amelia Alfonito (8) 111
Freddie Roberts (8) 112
Roksi Bhatti (9) 113
Emma Vulchera (8) 114
Olive Whyte (8) 115
Kit Henderson (9) 116
Olivia Harvie (11) 117
Matthew Duque Arcila (8) 118
Lola Wise (10) 119
Joshua Henderson (11) 120
David O'Connor (8) 121
Martina Formica (8) 122
Jenna Chu (11) 123
Bianca Giuliari (7) 124
Alexander Broomfield (8) 125
Uma Santaolalla (7) 126
Jean Carlos Orozco (8) 127
Cecilia Baiz Manthey (8) 128
Callum Graham (10) 129
Gonsague de Navacelle (8) 130
Katherine Brazdil (9) 131
Hannah Boffey (9) 132
Balthazar Demortreux (7) 133
Éléonore de Navacelle (9) 134
Ilaria Delargy (8) 135
Jannelle Chu (8) 136
Stella Burns (7) 137
Gregoire Cornet d'Elzius (9) 138
Jonah Nicola (8) 139
Izzy Adam (8) 140
Ted Slater (9) 141

LIPA Primary School, Liverpool

Nye Taylor (8) 142
Olive Carey-Rios (10) 143
Milah Waterfield (8) 144
Rowan Hodgkinson-Hillan (7) 145

St John's CE Primary Academy, Stafford

Zarah Gidman (11) 146

Christian Till (11)	149
Ayomide Olaseinde (11)	150
Abigail Hillis (11)	153
Chioma Anyanwu (11)	154
Lucas Rogers (11)	156
Jordon Phelps (11)	158
Iyla-Mai Crossley (11)	160
Nancy Bull (11)	162
Fraser Parsons (11)	164
Ernie Kenderdine (11)	165
Iyla Rose Copestake (10)	166
Devansh Pun (11)	168
Ore-Ofe Taiwo (10)	169
Phoebe Bull (11)	170
Lucas Brewis (11)	172
Himanthi Samaranayake (11)	174
Megan Barron (11)	175
Iyla-Rose Walters-Clark (11)	176
Alona Shinu (11)	178
Anusha Gurung (11)	179
Sarah Wright (11)	180
Zoe Parsons (11)	181
Baptiste Feliste (11)	182
Isabelle Pasquill (11)	183
Theo Middleton (11)	184
Noah Wrotchord (10)	185
Skyla Adams (10)	186
Ethan Harley (11)	187
Daniel Ross (11)	188
Ellie Booth (11)	189

Woodhouse Primary Academy, Quinton

Aisosa Lucky-Sunday (9)	190
Violet Stevens (9)	192
Toba Okunaiya (9)	193
Tammy Alao (9)	194
Mathieu Nkengni (9)	195
Courtney Francis (9)	196

THE CREATIVE
WRITING

The Galaxy Is Big

I dream about a flying dancer with dynamite in her hair,
She does dancing in the sky and flies everywhere.
She has a pretty pink tiara; she can turn around on one leg, that's really cool,
Make sure you catch her if she falls.
The famous footballer comes to have a play,
He's been kicking that football all day.
Monsters swim in dark swamps; they all pass me in the rainbow sky,
A royal horse passes by when I'm in the midnight sky.
Snakes coil around trees,
Trolls sunbathe in the breeze.
The galaxy is big, oh no, the sun is rising, I can't follow my dreams,
I'm waking up, it seems.
I eat my breakfast sadly, thinking about my dreams,
Goodbye, I'll see you next year, it seems.

Sophia Goodman (8)

Biscovey Academy, Par

Big Dreamer Time! (YouTube)

I like to put my life into a thought,
Where I shall be caught...
I sit in my aspiration,
Trying to rule the nation...

A dream can shoot to the moon,
Even if I'm in a cocoon...
My and your dreams shall be big,
As we get a better crib...

But a question might be,
What do I want to achieve?
A YouTuber or a mechanic,
Let's get at it...

A YouTuber's journey for 10,000,000 sub plaque,
Shall be hard, no cap.
A diamond plaque shall begin,
How is it with one sub in?

You won't get to success in a minute,
Even if you are good at cricket.
We shall dream, we can rise,
Maybe it will earn a good prize.

Well, we are taking little steps,
As we get good for what we get.
If you want to be famous, get a niece,
As your account decides to release.

Let's appreciate the fact that God gave us a chance,
To make us spread from LA to France.
So that's it, the end of the sheet,
And I can't wait for your channel release.

James Davies (11)
Biscovey Academy, Par

Night-Times

N othing looks like home in the dark of the night.

I hate night-time. I always get lost in my nightmares at night.

G lancing around at night, watching the moon.

H ow will I ever get to sleep?

T hud! Something moves in my wardrobe. What is creeping around?

T ime has struck midnight.

I s it a monster in my wardrobe?

M onsters don't exist. What am I thinking? Am I crazy?

E yes peek out of my wardrobe. I close my own in dread.

S uddenly, in the morning, I wake up to find I'm safe at home with Mum.

Paige Slaney (9)
Biscovey Academy, Par

My Spider Nightmare

Creepy-crawlies up my back,
Running around like a racing track.
Nightmares, a fate that I cannot escape,
So now picture a dream.
Little do I know as I walk down the street,
Miniscule insects silently creep behind me.
Even when I cross the street,
The spiders unexpectedly follow me.
They despise my life it ruins my cheer,
How can they do this with little to no fear?
So when life goes wrong just remember,
It's not just you in despair!
Sometimes it just might be you causing it to be unfair!

Mia Chubb (10)
Biscovey Academy, Par

Horror Baked Bean

Every night I have this dream,
But it's more of a nightmare it may seem.
I am being chased by a horror baked bean!
It is being awfully mean.
It keeps chasing me around the toast,
Catches me and I'm now a ghost.
Is this tomato sauce or is this blood?
This sauce is flowing like a flood,
Until I wake up with a sudden thud.
Now it's time to rise and shine,
Mum shouts up, "It's eating time!"
To the table, off I go,
Bacon, sausage... beans, oh no!

David Bolton (8)
Biscovey Academy, Par

6

Monsters

M edusa has deadly eyes and snakes as hair
O ff went the lights and it gave me a scare
N ow I start seeing snakes floating in the air
S ave me please, Medusa is there
T hen I hear hisses, it is just her hair
E arly in the morning, I see her again
R emembering she is actually my friend
S he hisses, then kisses me on the forehead.
Remember kids, monsters are your friends.

Jacob Mitchell (9)
Biscovey Academy, Par

Kindness

Once there was a girl
Who lived in a very big world
She found it oh so scary
Which made her oh so wary
But then, she made a friend
Which made her worries end
That's the good thing
That kindness can bring
And her friend, Ivy, said
"I promise that I will be kind and wave
Using my magic to help and save,"
And Olivia said
"Best friends forever."

Mya Mcdougall (7)
Biscovey Academy, Par

The Curse

Every day the curse lingered over my head
When I turned, I wanted to hide in my bed.

I was worried it was going to go on a spree
I wish I could be set free.

The only way to break the curse
Was to find the first Wendigo skull
Maybe it was hidden in a purse.

Theo Bourne (10)
Biscovey Academy, Par

My Dream

M y dream is to be a professional rugby player
Y et I'm still youth

D o I have the potential? Yes
R ugby player
E xeter, then England
A iming, I'm aiming
M otivated.

Ella Aldridge (11)
Biscovey Academy, Par

The Wolf Bird

The wolf is alone where no wolf should be,
He sits in the forest at the top of a tree.
I bought him some doughnuts and he flew down to me.
I said, "Don't eat them all cos you won't want your
tea!"

Betty Mitchell (9)
Biscovey Academy, Par

Fossils

In the woods and caves, we dig
Looking for fossils, small and big
On the hunt for dinosaur bones
We are breaking into the stones
Always excited for what we might see
Who will find it? My friends or me?

Jenson Barrott (8)
Biscovey Academy, Par

The Dream

I had a dream that started like this,
I went to see something that you could easily miss,
As I scurried through the thick grass,
I saw a sand-dripping hourglass.
What could this mean?
I'm not sure but it seems extreme...

Whilst I was running for my life,
I swear I saw a shadow of someone with a knife,
Suddenly, I lost my breath,
I thought, *will this be my death?*
As I was panting on the floor,
I looked up at the sky and there was a lot of gore,
Instead of rain, there were drips of blood,
Which were the colour of a rosebud,
Except it felt like mud,
Then I awoke back in the present.

Ella Gubby (10)
Brooksward School, Neath Hill

Dream Or Nightmare?

I'd heard the commotion from deep in the basement,
I stood up and went down even though it was out of
my placement.
Sinister cackles escaped from the room,
While I smelt obscure fumes.

I opened the door a little wider,
And there stood a witch whose face shone
recognisably brighter.
I stayed there for an hour since I had loads of time,
I thought they would soon get out so everything would
be fine.

I stood there for a little bit more,
Then I realised it was a quarter to four!
I flew into bed but I didn't go to sleep,
Then I woke up and realised it was all just a dream!
Or nightmare?

Aluna Mkono (9)
Brooksward School, Neath Hill

Royal Mess

I woke up in a luxurious room
Where am I?
My head was spinning like it was about to go *boom!*
A lovely lady smiled at me
She held my hand and led me somewhere
I asked her where could I be?
She grinned like a Cheshire cat
I was confused...
I found out on my head was a hat
Oh! It was a crown

I saw a grumpy lady
She gave me a glare
Looked quite shady
"Who are you?"
"I'm your mom"
Was this true?
I whispered, "More like a bomb"
The last thing I saw was a hand flying towards me.
Then I woke up...

Azizzah Akhtar (10)
Brooksward School, Neath Hill

The Forest Of Things Unexpected

A clean environment,
Rocks that start sediment.
The glistening stream trickled,
The ivy leaves prickled.
Then a few animals had a fight,
Will I ever see the light?
Suddenly, I got lost, maybe not found,
Perhaps, maybe a loud sound?
A very mysterious stone that shines,
On it, there were many lines!
Flowers that are dark,
Glum and dull parks.
Will I happily find my way,
Or will I forever stay...

Rumaila Rajabdeen (9)
Brooksward School, Neath Hill

This Is Me

Swim wild and swim free
There's a bright blue ocean ahead of me
On my own, I long to be
Peaceful and carefree
I swim, I dive, it's happiness for me
This is my escape from the struggles within me
It might seem I'm drowning, but I'm swimming free
This is my joy, inside of me
And this is my destiny, to be wild and free.

Ivy-Rose Lockey (10)
Brooksward School, Neath Hill

The Mystic Land

Once upon a land,
Lived some mystical creatures.
The evil trio,
George, Annabeth and Jamel.
They lived to tell this legend of...
Mother Earth.
Carol and Janet were the only hope,
To save this dimension.
Could they give this world,
What it takes,
To survive?

Maisy Chu (9)
Brooksward School, Neath Hill

A Mystical Land

I sat in my house
It was as quiet as a mouse
Suddenly, a wizard appeared
It gave me quite a fright
And then he disappeared out of sight
Then I went down a portal
I thought the wizard was immortal
Once I landed
I thought I was stranded
But there were waterfalls, dragons and fairies
And there were big, juicy cherries
Then I saw a dragon
He was full of passion
The wizard said his name was Spark
The wizard went to the park
So I was alone
Before the wizard went, he said his name was Simone
There was a sound I had never heard
It was books chirping like birds
Then I woke up in my bed
Realising it was all in my head!

Zaara Bibi (10)
Byron Primary School, Bradford

A Dream That Makes My Soul Scream!

One gloomy night, I wake up in a dark, gloomy bed
Suddenly I hear a bang, I think it is my brother Ken...
Nothing has prepared me for this strange land I see
I take a step forward, as nervous as can be...
Glancing left and right, all I see is smoke
How did I get here? I hope this is a joke
I go outside, I see fairies flying and dragons sleeping
I see pirates eating
And monsters slurping
Oh no, I am bleeding
I look down and see a little dragon munching on my feet
Suddenly my heart starts to beat
I see a cave and go to it
There is a scary dragon inside of it
The dragon wakes up and stares me in the eye
It starts to breathe fire
Running like Usain Bolt, it starts to give chase
I see a little fairy flying
"What happened little girl?" she says
"There is a fierce, scary dragon chasing me."

Eerie eyes glow, I close my own in dread...
Suddenly I wake up to find I'm safe at home in bed.

Ayesha Khan (10)
Byron Primary School, Bradford

The Yummy Crash

I went on a plane,
Everything was sane,
Until the plane crashed,
Everything got smashed,
I fainted,
It was like my eyes were painted,
I landed in the Macaroon Moors,
I could die because there were no doors,
I was starving so I ate a chocolate toadstool,
I didn't faint, but it was worse than freezing cool,
My stomach felt intense pain,
But, then a dragon came,
A big candy dragon that breathed candyfloss,
It was covered with a honey gloss,
It told me the chocolate monster was ruining its home,
And it started breathing fiery foam,
"You poor thing," I said sympathetically,
The monster seemed very deadly,
I flew to the monster,
For the dragon's honour,
It was very scary,
As scary as Bloody Mary,

Next, we took down the beast,
Now we can have a big macaroon feast,
I woke up from my dream,
But I saw white eyes that have never been seen,
Oh, it was my cat!

Sarah Khan (9)
Byron Primary School, Bradford

Scary Nightmares

One night I lie in my bed thinking about my dream,
Suddenly, I hear a scream,
I'm going to get a quick drink,
And I get sucked in!

Into a black hole,
I see a rolled-up scroll.
It says to look up,
A clown is screaming and it grunts.

I hear a monster coming near me,
Oh my gosh, there's three!
I find myself in a circus,
All the monsters look very nervous.

I see a dragon which is fiery and red,
I hope it's all in my head!
There's a scary spider and a magical wizard,
Thank god there's not a blizzard!

I see a flying superhero,
Whose number is zero!
She kills all of them,
She drops into my bed.
I wake up and look around.

I'm so hungry!
So I have some strawberries and cream!
Thank god it was just a dream...

Sofia Sajid (10)
Byron Primary School, Bradford

The Bear In The Air

After my nightmares every night,
I woke up full of fright...
Mum said to hang up the washing
But then I heard crashing
I looked up into the sky
I saw something fly
It wasn't just anything
It was a bear!
Eating my dad's underwear...
He took me with him
And we went for a swim!
It was all fun and games!
Until we saw flames...
There was a dinosaur in the pool!
The bear found it ultracool
The dinosaur was trying to eat me!
I knew I had to be free!
Then I woke up and realised it was just a nightmare...
But since then, I've never done the washing again!

Julia Wenio (9)
Byron Primary School, Bradford

The Magical Girl

Once, there was a girl
Who once learnt how to fly
She never ever knew she had powers
She was stunned
Since she figured out that she had magical powers
She decided to play, fly and twirl
She also rang her friends and taught them!
Once her friends came
They all flew one by one
Amazingly, the magical sky turned into candyfloss!
And they all began to eat it.
They thought it was delicious
Just like their magical world!
And when it rained the rain tasted like juice!

Saima Khalifa (10)
Byron Primary School, Bradford

Lost In Egypt

Once upon a dream on a hot, sunny day,
I fell asleep not to be seen,
I was in Egypt and the sun was steaming,
I was lost, well that's what I thought,
I saw famous people, righteous people, so many
people,
I was by myself with twelve shells,
It was really boring I started snoring,
The house was ginormous unlike a tortoise,
I started looking around but there was no sound,
It was so bright everything was out of sight,
It was such a good time hopefully I wake up to
sunshine.

Khawlah Khokhar (9)
Byron Primary School, Bradford

The Field And The Nearby Park

Through the field, met my cousin
Saw some flowers that showed their powers
Saw some grass as we passed
Looked at the weed with lots of plead.

Saw the blue sky while eating blueberry pie
Looking at the clouds made me feel proud
When I looked at the sky
I felt like I could fly.

Soon, we came across a park the size of Noah's Ark
I got flung when I swung on the swing
Loved to ride on the slide
When I was riding the see-saw, I said, "Yee-haw!"

Amayah Ali (10)
Byron Primary School, Bradford

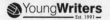
The Woods

As I walked into the woods and lifted my head
I felt calm that I wasn't surrounded by harm
When I saw a candy cane, a horse came
And showed off its mane
I ate a mango and let me tell you,
It was so divine that I lost my mind
As it swept me off my feet
(Because it was so sweet)
I left out some hay
And hoped that the horse would stay
However, my wish did not come true
And to top it off, I stepped in poo!
So, never come to the woods
Just eat Milk Duds.

Khadijah Sarwar (10)
Byron Primary School, Bradford

I Became A Bird

One ordinary day, I was flying a red vibrant kite,
All of a sudden, I started to gently float into the sky like a kite.
I became smaller and smaller!
I grew a small beak and feathery wings.

Suddenly, my skin felt like a soft pillow,
My small feet were like T-rex hands,
Then my mum shouted, "Wake up, you're going to be late for school!"
I woke up and realised it was a dream.

Yaqub Ahmed (10)
Byron Primary School, Bradford

The Night A Dragon Roamed My Room

As I slept,
I turned into a dragon.
My skin was as rough as tree bark,
My arms like a lizard,
My nails as sharp as lightning bolts.

My tail was like a crocodile's, dragging on the floor behind me.
My heavy wings lifted me into the air! I was frightened.
I felt like Icarus and waited to fall,
Losing control, I swooped down low and woke with a jump.

Essa Iqbal (10)
Byron Primary School, Bradford

Nightmares

Nightmares haunt me as I sleep
Then suddenly, I hear a beep
I walk outside and see a clown
He pulls and throws me into the water, so I drown
I swim to land and hide in the sand
He sees me so I run
He gives me a chase as the sun comes
I hide in bushes as the clown comes
He gets near me with guns
But I wake and I remember, it was just a dream...

Haytham Laher (10)
Byron Primary School, Bradford

My Special Unicorn Friends

When I go to sleep,
When I'm not to peep,
I wait until my mother tucks me in for the night,
All the thoughts in my head are bright
I take myself to a dreamland
My world, magic land with its candy cane castle,
Imps, fairies and pegasi are all in the bustle,
But the best magic thing, who lives in a cave,
Is a rainbow unicorn who I named Faith,
"Faith, hello, how are you?"
"Viola, you're back! I won't need the goo!"
"Then I ask, Faith, you...
Why did you say goo?"
She giggles and glories,
"It's a long story!"
Then over she comes, asking me to tea,
I say, "Yes, with honey from a bee!"
We have chips, burgers and ice cream on a plate,
Then I ask, over half a cup of milk,
"Faith, where is Ivy, with her hooves all wrapped in silk?
I'm feeling at the moment I won't see her
And I so want to feel her soft, soft fur!"

Then Faith says,
"Oh Viola, she's hiding away from rays,"
"But please can we visit her?
And her fur?"
Faith sighs, "Okay, I'll try." I pull myself upon her back,
And then we fly all through the black,

Until we see a little house,
And a candy-scurrying mouse,
She emerges, Eva too!
They all emerge all through the blue!
"Ivy let's fly out with you."

And as we fly, I see lots of new wonders,
Candy, cupcakes, waterfalls!
Candy chalked, muraled walls,
Rainbow, colourful, cosy houses!
Purple, candyfloss, running mouses!

Then Faith deftly hands me a key,
"Come on," she says, "This is the key,
And a bag in there with popcorn too,
And a marshmallow sandwich - whoo!"

And down we go to a little door,
And somehow I'm not touching the floor,
First I need to see why,
I'm not on the floor, oh my!
I've got a pair of shimmering wings,
Sparkling away like those rainbow torch things,

"Faith, here! Would you like a PJ?"
"Sure Faith, and now can I have a DJ?"
She goes to sort all
And I feel at the mall!
Sparkling, glimmering rainbow bushes,
Waving, swaying orange rushes,
Here, even the fire is green,
But there is more to be seen.

The sleeping bags,
They're not rags,
My bag's purple and blue,
And now, I hear a rainbow cow saying, "Moo!"
She means a lot to me,
Way more than just a bee
Then Faith says, "Tea? okay,
"Wait do I have to pay,"

I suddenly see Esra, a pony that I love,
I see Charlie! Here from heaven above,
And now I wake up,

I figure that I can't go back,
But a piece of my heart stays behind,
For my unicorn Faith to find.

Viola Dickson (8)
Chorister School (Durham Cathedral Schools Foundation), Durham

Behind The Waterfall

When I close my eyes,
I'm in a land of surprise.
You don't know what will happen next,
In the land of wonders.

But the biggest wonder of all,
Was a dazzling waterfall.
Stars and diamonds fall down,
From the waterfall in the land of wonders.

And often I wonder,
What lies behind the waterfall?
One day, I'll go, I'll go,
Beyond the land of wonders.

How suddenly I wake,
And forget the dream.
But next time, my heart knows,
I'll go through, through to the land beyond.

And now I go again,
I go behind, behind.
And now, I say,
"Goodbye, land of wonders."

O, the beauty of the land,
Magical, out of my dreams.
I feel welcome,
I'm in Dreamland, the land I love.

Then animals swarm around me,
My cats, my dead cats, Mephista,
George, Grace and Sandy.

The horses I love, Deacon, Jack,
Pepper, Toby, Frisby, Missy, Thomas,
Bob, Charlie, Kata, Bracken, Diamond,
Lena, Bonnie and the others.

And there,
The dream of my heart,
A horse, the greatest showjumper ever!

I'm in dreamland,
And I've found the missing piece of my heart!

Siri Ruerup (9)
Chorister School (Durham Cathedral Schools Foundation), Durham

Candyland

It's super sweet in Candyland,
The clouds are pink cotton candy,
The dogs play in the day,
The water is lemonade,
The dancers swirl and dance all night,
The birds swirl and twirl all day,
While a little boy, who has no name, hopes to go to space someday,
A little girl named Boe has an amazing life,
The homes are made of lollipops,
The sun is made of toffee,
A firework flies up in the sky and lights up like a huge night light,
Global warming does not exist here,
It's an amazing place to live,
I personally like the candy store, it has everything from big to small, thin to wide,
Anything good you can think of exists in Candyland,
Here the ice cream never melts.

Iona Macleod (9)
Chorister School (Durham Cathedral Schools Foundation), Durham

The Haunted Planet

I was walking around an eerie-looking world when suddenly, a witch came down and took me to her haunted mansion. It was flooded with ghosts and ghouls and zombies galore. It was like someone had packed Halloween into one house. The monsters were about to drop me into a pot of boiling water, when my dog, Spotty, came bounding in and all the monsters fled.

Spotty had saved me! Well, sort of... he didn't know how to untie the knot, but he did know how to bite the ropes away! I was free! But when I got out of the house, I met the witch again. She was going to cast a spell on me. That's when I woke up and realised that it was all just a dream.

James Kipling (9)
Chorister School (Durham Cathedral Schools Foundation), Durham

Princess Alicorn

P rancing through the palace.
R ipping through the trees.
I n the wobbly wood shouting!
N othing can stop me now!
C an't find home!
E nergetically shouting, "Where are you?"
S omething coming through the trees.
S omething scary

A terrified alicorn knows!
L eaving home is a bad idea.
I ncredibly, a monster jumps out of the bush!
"C ome here little alicorn."
"O h no, it's the monster called Death!"
R ipped his head off his body!
N ow to go back home!

Elizabeth Murray (9)
Chorister School (Durham Cathedral Schools Foundation), Durham

I Don't Want Peanut Butter For A Dragon

I don't want Nutella for a sister, she might get eaten
I don't want jam for a brother, he might go red in the face
I don't want sprinkles for a cousin, he might go rainbow and explode
I don't want a marshmallow for a mum, she might get big and big and melt in the microwave
I don't want a croissant for an uncle, he might get crispy and dry
I don't want peanut butter for a gran, she might get wrinkly
I don't want a lollipop for a dad, he will get sticky and sticky
I don't want ice cream for a grandad, he might melt
I don't want a Sour Patch Kid for a dragon, he might get sour.

Zara Moyes (9)
Chorister School (Durham Cathedral Schools Foundation), Durham

My Night Of Terror!

Have you ever thought of them?
The scary, horrid things!
They hunt you at night!
They're sure to give you a fright!
They go with a glimmer of light!
But once again, come back at the black of night.
Do you really want to go there?
It's like I'm seeing things from having too much beer!
It's puzzled me for many years!
How can I scream?
If it's just a bad dream!
Mum and Dad say I'm just sleep talking.
But what can they say about me walking?
Oh please! I've had enough!
Just wake me up!

Anae Ketani (8)
Chorister School (Durham Cathedral Schools Foundation), Durham

The Sun And The Moon

Once upon a time, there was a moon and a sun. The sun was handsome and happy, the moon was pretty and sad.
One day the sun wanted to meet the moon, but there were two sides, and the sun couldn't go to the side of the moon. They must find a way to meet. One of the boys told them what to do. So they did what the boy said, they pushed the two sides. But two was not enough, so the sun called all his villagers to push and push and the two sides became one side. The sun was going to marry the moon and there was a party and the moon became happy.

Moloko Bai (9)

Chorister School (Durham Cathedral Schools Foundation), Durham

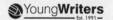

Robots Take Over The World

Robots work in every space,
Restaurants, hospitals and a fast food place,
Everywhere I go I can only find a robot,
I only want to find a human,
A person who's like me,
There's only me left, hopefully, one more, please,
If only I could bring back people,
Everyone would be fine,
Children playing in the streets,
Have fun alright,
Driving around everywhere,
Then I see a house,
A house with something in it,
A thing I thought had gone bye-bye,
People! I'm gonna be fine!

Douglas Pearson (9)
Chorister School (Durham Cathedral Schools Foundation), Durham

The Wizarding World!

W orld at war

I am hiding

Z enophilius got killed

A berforth is with me

R unning away from Death Eaters

D ead end, we turn

I disapparated!

N othing could stop us

G ood, I killed Voldemort!

W hat? He's still alive?

O h! Yes, I forgot to do the killing curse

R ight! Avada Kedavra!

L ay down or fell down into the lake

D ead! Whoop! Whoop! Avada Kedavra.

Elijah Wotton-Lidster (8)
Chorister School (Durham Cathedral Schools Foundation), Durham

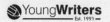

Nightmare Dragon

Once there was a land called Gems,
And there was a dragon with no friends.
Her name was Amethyst,
She was really in the mist.

She made friends with a dragon called Berry,
Over time she thought Berry was acting weird.
She thought nothing about it but then,
Berry kept twitching weirdly.

She said, "Berry are you okay?"
They started fighting and Berry got badly injured.
Amethyst woke up and realised,
It was a nightmare!

Julia Wilczek (9) & Emily
Chorister School (Durham Cathedral Schools Foundation), Durham

Midnight Skies

When you go to sleep and shut your eyes,
All you can see are the midnight skies,
Dreams can be happy and filled with glee,
And dreams can be dull and come quietly,
Dreams can be wonderful and filled with colour,
Or dreams can be grey (or even duller!)
Dreams can be reality or future or past,
But someday you'll get to the present, at last,
When you go to sleep and shut your eyes,
All you can see are the midnight skies!

Oliver Rayson (9)

Chorister School (Durham Cathedral Schools Foundation), Durham

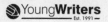

My Monster

My monster has sparkling spikes, glowing yellow eyes, pointy sharp fangs, nasty-looking claws, stinky breath like socks in manure and horns with claws on. Socks on its paws and its claws going through the socks, trees on its knees and very, very fluffy, and slow to catch its prey, without any nose, big wolf-looking eyes, hearts on his back, his tongue is split in half and it's mine, mine, mine!

Henry Hinton-Lee (8)

Chorister School (Durham Cathedral Schools Foundation), Durham

Dreams

D reaming of all the heavenly chocolate

R olo, Mars bar, Galaxy, KitKats, Twix and Snickers

E ating as many chunks of chocolate as I can

A mazed - they all appeal to me

M y mum and dad are also in my dream, they are eating all of my chocolate!

S ee you in my next dream.

Bella Allison Hood (9)

Chorister School (Durham Cathedral Schools Foundation), Durham

Space

S urprisingly, I have been teleported into a realm of darkness.
P lanets spin around me at the click of a finger
A liens run as fast as cheetahs
C ome over sometime, it's really fun!
E veryone is friendly here, we're just going in a moon buggy. Bye!

Joseph Adamson
Chorister School (Durham Cathedral Schools Foundation), Durham

My Mythical Dreamland

The golden, sticky lollipop sun gleamed
Through the cotton candy clouds.
The peppermint trees leapt with excitement
Grinning down at people
In a village, there is a chocolate fountain of wishes
Up on a mountain, there was a myth
Of a caramel waterfall.

Monty Campbell (9)
Chorister School (Durham Cathedral Schools Foundation), Durham

Nightmare Scare

Small, creepy ghosts haunt you at night,
That are going to give you a fright!
That will probably bite,
So be prepared to fight!
So hide under the blanket
Because he will find you!

Charles Spry (9)
Chorister School (Durham Cathedral Schools Foundation), Durham

Nightmare Scare

Small, creepy ghosts that haunt you at night
Are going to give you a fright
They will probably bite, so be prepared to fight
So hide under your blanket, because he'll find you
tonight!

Brody Maguire (9)
Chorister School (Durham Cathedral Schools Foundation), Durham

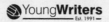

At Wembley

W inning
E xcitement
M emory
B eing happy
L oving the time
E njoying
Y ay, we scored.

Freddie Stonock (9)

Chorister School (Durham Cathedral Schools Foundation), Durham

The Circus Dream

I wake up one night and what do I see?
A colourful circus right in front of me.
I go in and I've missed the beginning.
A juggler's juggling and he's singing.

The next act is the weightlifter,
Who is the strongest of them all.
He does not know how to dance
And he has never been to a ball.

He lifts up a giant rock the size of a cow
And the magician comes in and says, "Kapow!"
He makes a balloon that looks like a dog
And makes it disappear in a cloud of fog.

Now that I've dreamt this dream,
Even though I like seabream,
I will dream this dream from now on
And it will feel like it is real.

Daydream Haiku:
Once upon a dream,
I dream of lovely horses.
Teacher wakes me up.

Kareem Bizzari (9)
Fulham Preparatory School, London

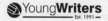

Panic

Once, when my head hit the pillow,
I dreamed of standing with tall, dark willows,
I was stranded there, left alone,
With nothing to guide me home.
Then I was stuck in a huge merciless city,
With nobody around to help or pity,
Suddenly, I was falling off a cliff!
Down below, crocodiles waited with mouths that would devour me in a piff!
I closed my eyes, hoping for the best...
And I opened them to find myself in bed!

Diego Muran Zha (9)
Fulham Preparatory School, London

My Dream Is My World

The world is what you make of it.
Or is it a dream, what do you think of it?

I saw a fish that could fly.
What a joy to reach the sky!

You know it rains when the sky-taps are leaking.
Oh no! I saw a lonely cloud weeping!

I saw a sun who takes a bath daily.
So that his hair doesn't look wavy!

Now this is the world, what I think of it.
Or is it a dream, what do I make of it?

Muhammad Hadi Aziz (8)
Fulham Preparatory School, London

Llama Problems

Sometimes in my dreams, I dream that I am a llama.

I'm a special kind of llama
In a special llama shower
Singing special llama songs
With a special llama flower
Doing special llama poses
In a special llama school
Dancing special llama moves
In a special llama pool
Using special llama tools
Like a special llama cool
But my special llama problem...
I that I am actually a fool.

Josephine Kolmahov (9)
Fulham Preparatory School, London

Star Teamwork Climb

When I climbed Mount Everest
My heart shone brighter
There, I saw the sunset
And the dark of the night stars
The next day we climbed down the mountain
And we saw some sparks,
It was a unicorn, she took our horse back home
And we saw a fountain on the next mountain
There was a party and there was a climber race
And we... won!

Emma Aparici (8)
Fulham Preparatory School, London

Howling Horror Hunt

Forest dreaming
Calm relaxing
Claws hiding
Head worrying
Wolf sprinting
Panic rising
Hill dashing
Mouth shouting
Claw scratching
Blood pouring
Eyes nearing
Heart pounding
Teeth approaching
Jaws opening
Sudden waking
Nightmare ending.

Celia Zhang (8)
Fulham Preparatory School, London

Creepy Creature Chase

Park walking
Calm strolling
Spider hiding
Fear rising
Legs speeding
Heart beating
Feet stomping
Horror coming
Claws scratching
Pain worsening
Feet trembling
Mind racing
Jaws trapping
Blood pulsing
Sudden waking
Nightmare ending.

Maica Chiou (8)
Fulham Preparatory School, London

Rattling Ribcage Race

Classroom dreaming
Gentle sleeping
Teacher changing
Fear starting
Bones appearing
Heart racing
Toe stubbing
Wound hurting
Head bleeding
Blood pouring
Skeleton nearing
Shock rising
Sudden waking
Nightmare ending.

Clement Bulmer (8)
Fulham Preparatory School, London

Nightmare Of The Nimble

Tree dreaming, calm sleeping
Nose sneaking, heart beating
Fox pouncing, panic rising
Arms quivering, lungs screaming
Teeth crunching, blood spilling
Body sprinting, legs aching
Claws jumping, eyes closing
Sudden waking, nightmare ceasing.

Summer Greenland (8)
Fulham Preparatory School, London

Terrifying Tail Chase

Mountain hiking
Happy laughing
Dragon lurking
Anger appearing
Fire chasing
Fear racing
Cave jumping
Heart stopping
Arm twisting
Bone breaking
Teeth hearing
Jaws closing
Sudden screaming
Nightmare ending.

Ameen Yaqoob (8)
Fulham Preparatory School, London

Scary Sprint Saga

Sunbathing, sleepy snoring;
Elephant chasing, panicked running;
Trunk storming, frightened puffing;
Tree climbing, head sweating;
Tusks destroying, heart rising;
Feet fading, fear disappearing;
Eyes opening, nightmare fading.

Vincent Wang (8)
Fulham Preparatory School, London

Shadowy Spirit Sprint!

Bed dozing, gentle dreaming;
Door creaking, fear building;
Shadow running, heartbeat racing;
Ghost chasing, fright closing;
Knee cracking, agony rising;
Hands nearing, terror closing;
Sudden waking, nightmare ending!

Amelia Sethi (8)
Fulham Preparatory School, London

Cursed Creature Chase

Early morning.
Clouds glooming.
Teeth chattering.
Lips drying.
Claws chasing.
Heart beating.
Rapid falling.
Ankle twisting.
Mouth opening.
Silent screaming.
Eyes opening.
Nightmare ending.

Hadi Tabib (8)
Fulham Preparatory School, London

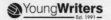
Zombies, Frightful, Run!

Fun gaming
Happy playing
Zombie running
Fear rising
Arms grabbing
Heart beating
Zombie scratching
Back cracking
Monster hiding
Scared sprinting
Sudden waking
Nightmare ending.

Cooper Campbell (8)
Fulham Preparatory School, London

Fleeing From Fear

Park resting
Wonderful dreaming
Wolf prowling
Panic building
Pond jumping
Sweat dripping
Leg cracking
Pain growing
Claws nearing
Eyes widening
Sudden yelling
Nightmare ending.

Yunuo (George) Song (8)
Fulham Preparatory School, London

Panic And Pursuit

Dog walking
Calm jogging
Bark calling
Heart beating
Ghost appearing
Fear building
Scared cunning
Worry rising
Leg bleeding
Sweat dripping
Sudden waking
Nightmare ending.

Hedda Husvaeg Derome (8)
Fulham Preparatory School, London

Army's Angry Advance

Game playing
Home chilling
Army hiding
Fingers trembling
Body shaking
Heart beating
Tanks rumbling
Legs sprinting
Eyes opening
Nightmare ending.

Nico Turney (7)
Fulham Preparatory School, London

My Dream

Once upon a dream,
I had this little dream,
Where I wanted to scream,
But this scream stopped screaming,
Then, finally, my dream came true,
So now I get to scream.

Theo Asghar (7)
Fulham Preparatory School, London

Rainbow Land

Rainbow Land is colourful and bright, with trees growing upside down and leaves shaped like love hearts. There are flowers growing everywhere, the houses are shaped like shoes and the shoelaces are used as slides, with the silly, joking fairies playing all around and making funny noises.

I suddenly find myself in Rainbow Land and one of the silly fairies is holding my hand! The fairy asks me, "Are you coming in your pyjamas to the silly fairies' grand show in the magical world of Rainbow Land?"

I look at her very amazed and answer, "Why am I here? Can I have a dress for the occasion then?"

The fairy leads me to the fairy flower valley and with a *whoosh*, a heap of red poppies shape themselves into a beautiful ballgown which I wear, very amazed, at the fairy show.

I suddenly hear my mum's voice calling for breakfast and think what a wonderful dream. Mmmm, can I go back to the fairy show?

Emma Marie Scicchitano (8)
Holy Ghost Catholic Primary School, Wandsworth

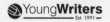
The Wizard Tower

My eyes jerked open as my legs tumbled beneath me, forcing me to the floor. It was cold and wet, strange to me as I had never felt that sensation before. Where was I? Where was I before this? Though even if I rocked it as hard as I could, my brain was empty. I looked up, it was so strange, eerie. In front of me was a completely black forest only inhabited by blotches of grey strewn across the many trees. I shook to my feet, my eyes wandering around the many trees, they wandered a little up to the violet sky, which instead of a setting sun, was a concealing moon. Not wanting to stay in this weird place for too long, I set into the dark forest which was looming in front of me daring me to come in.

As soon as I set foot into the forest, a great roar reached my ears as an explosion of fire broke the sky. Then a cackle as if a wizard was here. I had always wanted to see a wizard. You could say it's one of my life goals. Then, there it was again, it was closer now, louder now. The nostalgia of me playing wizard with my little brother in the garden, him shouting happily, me singing kindly to him as we threw spells at each other.

Finally, reaching a great tower with old-fashioned stones lining all around it. As I called up, all that reached me was a great roar. Then I felt a wave of relief wash over me and I woke up panting in my bed!

Izzy Pass (11)
Holy Ghost Catholic Primary School, Wandsworth

The Forest Of My Dreams

Every evening, amongst a swirling, misty haze and a
pitch-black sky with bright twinkling eyes dotted
around;
Echoing through the night is a loud hooting sound;
I conjure up a myriad of dreams, but they only make
way for one;
Starting with me, in the depths of the vast, ancient
forest of secrets, under the sun;
I lie down on a carpet of foliage; looking up unravels a
canopy of pea-green, khaki trees;
And I see flying rainbows, hanging around in threes;
I resume strolling around in the gnarled, twisted vines;
I explore and investigate a variety of tracks, where
creatures used to roam in lines;
Suddenly, the path veers to the left and I have a
fleeting view revealing a vivid, sapphire, flowing ribbon,
Acting as a threshold for the north and south, being
weather-driven;
All of a sudden, *roar!*
I realise there is a beautiful lion, towards me he soars;
Nothing to do, so I take last glimpses of the majestic
trees standing tall and proud;
Which join together to form a crowd of vivid green
umbrellas, whispering to themselves, an eerie sound;

Suddenly, *crash!* Over for now;
And I wake with a jolt, I hope only to wait until my next sleep, not being sent back with a growl...

Arun Agostinelli (9)

Holy Ghost Catholic Primary School, Wandsworth

Haunted

She walks along the corridors,
Nobody knows she's there,
She looks out every window,
Pacing each floorboard with care.

She wanders alone like a ghost,
She looks so very lost,
She doesn't bother to make friends,
Each friendship has a cost.

She is the school phantom,
A loner, a misfit,
The whispering white lady holding a lantern,
The lantern that is always lit.

Nobody loves her,
Nobody cares,
She darts behind the stage,
She hides under the stairs.

The only thing she understands is hiding,
Hiding from life, hiding from her memories,
The memories that haunt her sleep.

Everything is fuzzy and unclear,
She wipes her eyes and steadies her tears,
She wishes she could just disappear,
Or at least get rid of her fear.

She wants all of this to just be a dream,
But dreams aren't trustworthy,
They're not what they seem.

All the thoughts taunt her,
Multiplying her dread,
Soon the only things left of her,
Will be the books she's read.

She takes out a crossword, clicks her pen once,
Nine across, a bad or haunting dream.
Nightmare.

Giulia Galtieri (10)
Holy Ghost Catholic Primary School, Wandsworth

Untitled

Here I am one spring day in May in the Old Trafford
football ground with crowds and crowds all around.
I am in the very last minute, last game and we are
chasing fame.
I'll keep putting a hand on the ball after the opponent's
wake-up call,
With incredible skill Jacob runs into space.
The keeper has seen him and wallops the ball.
With astonishing skill, Jacob gathers the ball from the
air, he sees me and we are a pair.
We're in midfield and it's so far to go I've got to get
forward, so he can pass me the ball.
Jacob cannot fail, there's someone on his tail.
Jacob launches the ball from way out left, I'm on the
edge of the box waiting to pounce and in an instant it
lands at my feet with a single bounce.
Suddenly the game ignites into flames as the fans
chant my name, it's now or never, it's time for an
outswing.
As I pivot to my right I smash it into the air like a jet it
lands first outwards then inwards into the back of the
net.
The ref's final whistle signals the end of the match.
We've done it.

But wait, there's a catch, before I know it, the roars of the crowd fade as I awake today, it's all been a dream...

Hugo Herburt-Burns (9)

Holy Ghost Catholic Primary School, Wandsworth

Dreams Of Handstands And Cartwheels!

As I close my eyes and fall asleep;
Many dreams whirl around my head but only one
remains deep;
I find myself surrounded by millions cheering;
I'm in my favourite place but what I'll have to perform I
find a little fearing;
I squint my eyes as I stare at the colourful leotards with
shimmering gems;
The competition's about to begin, we walk full of
excitement to the bars, enemies now but after friends;
Swinging confidently from bar to bar, the swirling chalk
drifts down like snow falling from the sky;
I blush bright red, I was full of nerves, but it was my
best try;
Next up the floor, roller coaster cartwheels across the
mat and cat leaps with knees to chest;
My routine is perfect, just a stumble as I spin in a spiral
and come to rest;
The judges seem impressed, did I do enough to win? As
I wait, I jump;
The scores are up, my heart is beating like a pump;

I step onto the golden shiny podium, proud;
As I get my trophy, cheers booming from the crowd;
A wide smile lights up my delighted face;
My dreams has come true, I've won first place!

Kyla Agostinelli (7)
Holy Ghost Catholic Primary School, Wandsworth

Adventure Of A Lifetime

I am Christopher Columbus,
I'm on a journey around the world.
Oh no! A powerful storm is on its way,
We don't have time to run away!
The sea is dark, I have been struck and turned into a
piece of foam.
I'm lifted into freezing air,
I feel as light as a piece of hair.
And suddenly, I realise I've travelled back in time!
Surprise!
I'm really, truly, quite amazed to meet small creatures
face-to-face!
"We are Oompa Loompas by the way!
We have a project on its way
You, stranger! Help us save the world from danger!"
I fly with them up to the sky,
Where magic spells are passing by,
And dropping to the land below.
The fire stops, the storm calms down,
And suddenly I turn around,
And with the help of a magic spell,
I safely travel back to land.

I find myself on a steady ship,
With no more danger on my trip!

Alex Catalogna (8)

Holy Ghost Catholic Primary School, Wandsworth

The Flying Circus

I close my eyes and suddenly, *pop*, I'm in the circus,
With mouth-watering sweets,
And cotton candy in the shape of animals,
The popcorn glitters in the evening sunshine.
I go into an enormous red and white striped tent,
There are about one thousand seats,
The arena stands in the middle proudly,
The lights flicker off and the show begins.
Horses gallop round and round,
Gymnasts backflip around the side,
Strong men lift three fully grown men at the same time.
All of a sudden, the circus starts rocking from side to side,
It's flying, *bump* it lands.
Everyone empties out but different people this time,
The mysterious land looks magnificent,
I try to step out to see the houses made of sweets but I can't.
I blink and when I open my eyes again I am back in my room,
Where is the circus?
Was it a dream?

Maeva Moore (8)
Holy Ghost Catholic Primary School, Wandsworth

Dreaming Tonight

D are I rest my head,

R est my tired eyes,

E ventually, I do, blinking through tries.

A fter I enter my head,

M y brain whizzes, pops and does a slight hop.

I feel intrigued; interest and adventure fill me and enter my body,

N ow I stand alone, just me, until a buzzing bee approaches me,

G radually, followed by graceful fairies all around.

T hen, a hill suddenly appears with the fairies escorting me,

O ut of nowhere. When I reach the top, a river with my voice trails,

"N arwhal!" I cry. There in a shimmering lake, it awaits me.

I step forward, it swims forward,

G ently, I take its hand and offer to stroke it.

H opeful, I squeeze my eyes shut, too nervous to look,

T hen, when I open them, I am greeted to the morning sun of the day.

Eibhlin Reynolds Paul (9)
Holy Ghost Catholic Primary School, Wandsworth

Flying At Night

In my bed every night
I see carpets of darkness splattered with white
The shimmering shell stands
Proud and high
It is my favourite time of night
You might be wondering why.

With the gentle breeze blowing against my face
The smell of freedom is all I can taste
Like a golden eagle gliding in the scarlet night
While my chest is filled with a burning light!

As the city is tired from the day before
All the buildings begin to snore
Below me, houses with tiles of protective shields
While, beside it, dewy grass spreads over fields

I fly up high for hours and hours
My senses alive, I feel I have powers
Until the blazing sun kisses the dark sky with gold
It's now time to go home, I am told
Soaring over cities, buildings and even my shed
I open my eyes to find myself, cosy, in bed.

Millie Wittet (10)
Holy Ghost Catholic Primary School, Wandsworth

The Stars

I look out of the window at night,
I see stars shining so very bright,
I wonder what life there might be in the stars,
And what would I do if I was up near Mars,
I would be able to see the whole world,
And what my parents and family were doing,
And see people from every country and every
nationality.
I might be able to stop all the wars and prevent conflict
Or maybe simply invite others to the bright stars,
To help them see the world as I see it.
I might even be able to find some more life in the stars.
Could there be a new race or religion to be discovered?
Or simply little green Martians or aliens,
Going about their daily routines?
Either way, it is a mystery to me,
As I look up and wonder what might be up there,
Next to the stars so bright.

Eva Molloy (8)
Holy Ghost Catholic Primary School, Wandsworth

Magic Sweet Shop Dream!

M ysterious place you end up in.
A mazing sweets everywhere.
G iants are even made from sweets.
I ncredibly the candyfloss clouds burp.
C rumbling houses ready to be eaten.

S weets galore.
W obbly jelly on a spoon.
E xtraordinary things happen.
E xchanging money for delicious sweets.
T ingling taste in the mouth.

S hops made of sweets everywhere.
H oping sweets keep coming.
O pening boxes of chocolates, soft and gooey.
P ops from the freezer, icy and cold.

D ream magic happening.
R unning, eating sweets.
E ntering a new land.
A nd now it is all over.
M agic.

Harry Young (7)
Holy Ghost Catholic Primary School, Wandsworth

Shadow Clowns

I sprint down this dark tunnel,
Shadow Clowns on my tail,
My heavy breathing is racking my bones,
The Shadow Clowns creeping along,
They emerge from the shadows,
Red teeth, I wonder how they turned that colour,
A shiver goes down my spine as they edge closer,
I can see its cold, deadly breath,
And I know that any moment could be my last,
I think about happy memories,
A smile creeps across the ugly beast's face.

Suddenly, a high-pitched whistle sounds,
The beast covers its ears and falls to the ground,
At that moment I knew it was over,
There was a scent of his blood in the air,
But there was also victory!

Olann Pearce (9)
Holy Ghost Catholic Primary School, Wandsworth

Old Lady Policia

In London, ten years long,
The Old Lady Policia has worked,
Arresting 800 old ladies,
Some of them very dangerous.

For help, dial 991
To report an emergency.
Here are some well-known stories about these old ladies:

They use cake guns,
Aimed at your empty stomach,
Their target is your mouth.

Highly trained in giving hugs,
Best not to mess with them.
They tell us they can help any time with their wise old words,
Try it! Call them for an occasional chat.

We dreamers love these old ladies,
They escape, buy us ice creams and never tell us off.

They're like a dream come true!

Daniel Kaiza (9)
Holy Ghost Catholic Primary School, Wandsworth

Lost

I dreamed I walked through a forest in my gloomy nightmare. It was dark and I was not scared, when I began to see abandoned statues, hard as metal, covered in moss, I was confused and realised I was lost! A dancer appeared dancing around with hair of flowers and beautiful things, glistening clothes, twinkling like stars. She brightened the way and told me not to be scared. As everything started to light with fairy jars, I found my way with the dancer. Fairy lights danced brightly as we played and then there was a faint smell I knew. It drew me forward, what was it? I had to go! It smelled like sizzling, it smelled like bacon! I was giggling! Bacon? That meant it was breakfast!

Mariana Stephenson (8)

Holy Ghost Catholic Primary School, Wandsworth

Wild And Free

Here I stand.
I stand among these amazing creatures that roam the world.
I feel calm, peaceful and loved.
I sense the amazing wilderness flowing into my oesophagus.
I feel a small tickle up my spine to find a butterfly resting
as gracefully as a swan on my shoulder.
I smell the dazzling perfume of the roses that lie above me.
I see the tall gargantuan tree majestically towering over me.
Suddenly, I feel the ground quivering as if it felt cold,
I find that I am being chased by a restless unicorn.
I panic, too scared to even run,
But then the unicorn smiles and pops me on her back and escorts me out of my dream world...

Isabella Diana (9)
Holy Ghost Catholic Primary School, Wandsworth

The Midnight Dream

As I lie in my bed,
Cosy and warm,
I gaze at my window,
Staring at the beautiful night sky, I thought,
Shooting stars are like little pixies floating about,
Planets are like big balloons floating about,
But what's beyond the solar system?
My sister told me a fine little tale...
Petite monsters are doing a hard job,
The Questioner goes into your head and says,
did I leave the stove on?
Dreamo helps you dream.
As I think I see a bright blue blob soar in and out of the houses –
I'm utterly confused but before I can think...
I get put to sleep...
A mystery I can't solve!

Elizabeth Wells (10)
Holy Ghost Catholic Primary School, Wandsworth

The Girl On The Beach

I wake up from the most exquisite dream about me on a beautiful beach,
That's how I imagine it. I get up from my bed and change, then I go downstairs to have breakfast. I suddenly realise that there is a place that I can go to that is special and peaceful, the beach!
I pack my travelling stuff and run out of the front door. I take the bus to the most brilliant beach that I can find!
Two hours later, I'm at the beach, I can see the waves sweeping back and forth, I sit down and grab a drink!
I take my shoes off and dip my feet in the water as I hear the birds tweet!
The luscious blue water laps round my legs, I feel so relaxed!

Amelia Jackson-Dauncey (10)
Holy Ghost Catholic Primary School, Wandsworth

The Terrible Clown

Every day, we go to sleep and we have dreams, but not every dream is scary.

The patient is patiently waiting for the visitor to come, but this isn't the visitor he was expecting. It is a clown with red and white cheeks.

The nurse goes tiptoeing like a squirrel. It is now only the patient and the clown. In a matter of seconds, the clown brings a weapon and hides under the bed.

The patient is starting to panic and feels like he is going to faint. He begins screaming like a roaring tiger. He hears footsteps and sees a weapon coming out of the bed. He starts to tremble, but...

I found out that I was safe at home.

Richard Matuszewski (9)
Holy Ghost Catholic Primary School, Wandsworth

Run, Run, Run

Run, sprint, race
This is the wish I want to chase
When I run, I feel buoyant and free
And that is all I want to be.

Run, run, run
Faster, faster.

On your marks, get set, go!
At first, I think I am rather slow
The wind in my face, my arms moving fast
This is so much fun; I am having a blast!

Run, run, run
Faster, faster.

I don't run to win; I run to achieve
I can do anything, I want to believe
The sound of my feet, pounding the road
And the thought of winning, surges and flows.

Run, run, run
I am the fastest.

Eva Wittet (10)
Holy Ghost Catholic Primary School, Wandsworth

Inside Van Gogh

Every time I fall asleep,
I remember a summery field of wheat.

Yellow, thick and bright,
With cypresses, flowers and hay very tight.

Whipped cream in the azure sky,
Makes me eager to try and fly.

Outside of the vase under the scorching sun,
I pick sunflowers and I start to run.

Softly, a cobalt night painted above me,
Whirls and twirls to set me free.

Radiant glowing stars dance in the space,
Making a move with harmony and grace.

All around, my bedroom sparkles and gleams,
I dream of painting and then I paint my dream.

Giorgio Gambacorta (9)
Holy Ghost Catholic Primary School, Wandsworth

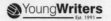

The Magnificent Race

I heard the crowd cheering everybody's name. It was like a mega-trumpet playing in my ear. Suddenly, I heard the start, "Ready, set, go!"
My legs started pounding and ten seconds had passed, 400 metres to go. I had to focus. 200 metres to go. Another racer was catching up. 100 metres to go. I needed to beat the USA to win. 50 metres were left. I had to sprint harder than I had ever sprinted before. It was the end of the race. I ran it in sixty-six seconds. The commentator said it was a new world record! I laughed in joy while I celebrated my glory. I shook the other competitors' hands in disbelief!

Garance Roch (9)
Holy Ghost Catholic Primary School, Wandsworth

A Dream Across The Universe

Once upon a dream,
I went out of this world.
I was launched up into space,
Like a rocket,
The stars danced around me.
I watched a show on Venus,
Then, picnicked on Jupiter.
On Saturn, I skateboarded,
And on Uranus, cycled.
On Mars, a football match was on,
And on Mercury, it was the first day
After the holiday.
On Neptune, I lit the Olympic flame,
And afterwards, I jumped back to Earth,
To pull myself out of my dream,
The day flew by,
The night said, "Hi."
The dreaming gates opened,
What would my next dream be?

Aliénor Demortreux (9)
Holy Ghost Catholic Primary School, Wandsworth

I Had A Dream

I had a dream that I was standing in McDonald's and I wanted a Big Mac because I was hungry. Then I asked for a Big Mac.

They said, "We don't sell it here now."

Oh McDonald's, why did you do that? Oh, McDonald's, why did you do that? Oh McDonald's, why did you do that? Oh, McDonald's. They told me I should go to KFC so I travelled 10 miles to KFC then I asked for my Big Mac.

They said, "What? We don't do it here."

Oh KFC, why did you do that? Oh KFC, why did you do that? Oh KFC, why did you do that? Oh KFC...

Joella-Eden Asamoah (11)
Holy Ghost Catholic Primary School, Wandsworth

Dreams

I dream to be an astronaut, to be the first woman on Mars,
To touch the planet with my own hands, I know I can reach for the *stars!*
I dream of meeting a unicorn, touching its soft white mane,
I wish to live in unicorn land, wow, that would be *insane!*

I dream to be a writer, to write books for the world,
To write poems about parties and how ballerinas twirled,

But I would like to be everything, and that's just fine,
I've got a whole life ahead of me and like a star, I'll *shine!*

Angelica Adami (9)
Holy Ghost Catholic Primary School, Wandsworth

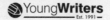

The Beach

I saw the tall, vast trees swaying in the wind. The sun was as bright as a spotlight. Birds chirped with joy and the smooth pebbles were as smooth as a newborn baby's skin. The sand was as hot as a burning oven. The animals splashed in the sea, splish, splash.
Every day I walk on the sand so that I never have a bad dream in my life. I skip all day long on the sand. Every night I would stay up late to go down the light blue slide made out of rubber and air. But, sadly, they all just disappear out of this world. Maybe on holiday, it will really happen.

Haizea Waterworth (8)
Holy Ghost Catholic Primary School, Wandsworth

Champions

C rowds are cheering, singing and applauding,

H appy and heroic footballers scoring!

A n interesting match is taking place,

M illions are glued to watch the players' speedy pace!

P rayers are sent for every kick,

I mportant goals are being kicked.

O mnipotent strikers shooting from the middle of the pitch,

N evertheless, the whole game went without a hitch.

S uddenly, the referee blew the whistle and the opponents bristled because we were the *champions*!

Etienne Conti (8)

Holy Ghost Catholic Primary School, Wandsworth

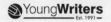

Football

Football is my favourite game
I love to watch them play
Amazing players playing
On an awesome autumn day
How fluidly and gracefully
They dance across the green
Such elegant contenders play
The best I've ever seen.

Some people think I'm crazy
The way I love the game
But I'd rather be watching football
Than anything I can name
Of course, I may be prejudiced
I love my maise and blue
The big ten teams that rule the league
You rock the big house blue!

Dylan Medeiros (10)
Holy Ghost Catholic Primary School, Wandsworth

Harry Potter Dream

I find myself in Hagrid's hut,
Happy, gloomy, not quite sure,
Could be either, what do you think?
Harry walks around the table, not sure what to do,
Suddenly he shouts, "Aha, ahoo,
Listen to my plan, we need Hagrid to track down Aragog,
So we can turn him into a cute little bunny,
Then he will cause us no more harm and we can live in peace."
"Danny, Danny, what do you like to build in Minecraft?"
"Ted!" I groan. "I was having an exciting dream!"

Danny Slater (7)
Holy Ghost Catholic Primary School, Wandsworth

I Don't Ask For The Moon

I feel as light as a feather
My feet don't touch the ground
I'm free to wander further and further
All the way to my favourite playground.

I don't need wings to soar up high
My legs carry me. Run, jump, go!
I never reach the bright blue sky
Beneath the streetlights, I am floating quite low.

I can stay up there for as long as I like
The big, bad wolf will never catch me
I'm fast asleep. I smile in the moonlight
Small things make me happy.

Sofia Fattouche (7)
Holy Ghost Catholic Primary School, Wandsworth

A Trip Into A Forest

Once upon a time, there was a girl that set off into the woods,
but accidentally went off the trail and got lost deep into the woods!
The girl stopped and crouched down with tears, she then heard a sound and was very curious, so she got up and searched for whatever was making the sound.
It was a lovely hummingbird flapping its wings, she was amazed!
She went deeper into the woods and saw a lovely bird!
When she saw all the animals, she found her way back home and had cake with her mum!

Amelia Alfonito (8)
Holy Ghost Catholic Primary School, Wandsworth

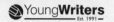

A Way To A Good Dream

The sun is black,
The moon is bright,
Now I can see that it is night.

Outside in the city, shadows of every kind,
Conjure up feelings of sadness and horror in my mind.

Tonight, will I dream of winning millions of pounds,
Or will I dream of troubles and frowns?

I'll think about the things that make me glad,
And push away the feelings that make me sad.

Now we can see there is nothing to fear,
Going to sleep is a good idea.

Freddie Roberts (8)
Holy Ghost Catholic Primary School, Wandsworth

The Blue Monster Man!

Look out! Look out! There is a blue monster man about! The blue monster looks like a traveller and he mysteriously wanders everywhere.
I feel so petrified. The blue monster is chasing us! As the blue monster man approaches us, he reaches my old friend's hair and, in the blink of an eye, my old friend's hair turns white. Then he shocks my hands with a taser so my hands turn brown!
The blue monster man gifts me a card that says 'a deal is a deal!' Then he suddenly disappears.

Roksi Bhatti (9)
Holy Ghost Catholic Primary School, Wandsworth

I Woke Up This Morning

I woke up this morning at quarter past seven
I tidied up the covers and stuck out my toe
My dream was about a night that will never stay
The night will never stay
The night will still go by even if a bird rushes down in my eye
Through a million stars you pin to the sky
Though you blind it with the moon
The night will slip away like a bird's tune
I stay in bed, I don't care
At quarter past eight they can get me
But I'm staying in bed!

Emma Vulchera (8)
Holy Ghost Catholic Primary School, Wandsworth

114

Daydreaming

D ancing with my closest friends
A t a fancy gala in the woods
Y ellow daffodils fill vases on the table
D resses in colours of pink and blue
R eminding me of candyfloss
E veryone is happy
A s they dance around the room
M oving elegantly
I cing gently covers several cakes
N ow I hear my teacher calling my name
G et back to work, daydreaming has ended.

Olive Whyte (8)
Holy Ghost Catholic Primary School, Wandsworth

Paws For Thought

As I, Colonel Meow, promenade down the garden
With the sun warming my fur, the wind tickling my
whiskers
The moist green grass in-between my toe beans
This is the life for me
Taking up my rightful position on top of the fence
I can observe my kingdom below
Many battles await
Mice to be caught!
Birds to be pawed!
Next-door's dog to be terrorised!
But first, a nap
A cat's work is never done.

Kit Henderson (9)
Holy Ghost Catholic Primary School, Wandsworth

Hot 'N' Cold

Hot is the thing that makes me sick,
Hot is the thing my head gets when I'm jealous,
Hot is the thing my hands get when I'm guilty,
Hot is the thing that the sun makes me,
Hot is the thing that makes me, me.
But...
Cold is the thing that makes me numb,
Cold is the thing that I feel when I'm sad,
Cold is the thing that makes icebergs form,
Cold is the thing that makes everything seem bad!

Olivia Harvie (11)

Holy Ghost Catholic Primary School, Wandsworth

A Boy Sleeping And A Spider's In The Boy's Nose

When the boy is sleeping, a spider goes in his nose. Suddenly, the boy wakes up and realises that there is a spider in his nose. The boy tells his mum and dad and the boy's dad tries to get the spider. The boy's dad can't do anything so the dad calls 999 and the ambulance and tells them what is happening. The ambulance rushes to the hospital and they check the boy and they get the spider out of the boy's nose and the boy is okay.

Matthew Duque Arcila (8)
Holy Ghost Catholic Primary School, Wandsworth

Darkness

D anger lurks around the corner,

A s I took a step forwards a sound came from behind me,

R attle, rattle, rattle, rattle, rattle, rattle,

K nowing that I couldn't cry for help, I stood still,

N ot daring to breathe,

E very hair on the back of my neck stood up,

S omething touched my shoulder,

S uddenly I woke up but something was still touching my shoulder.

Lola Wise (10)
Holy Ghost Catholic Primary School, Wandsworth

Thief

I creep out of the doorway,
And tiptoe down the hallway.
I glance nervously behind me,
Holding my urge to flee.

I have come this far,
I can't go back.
If anyone comes after me,
I will attack.

The mission I have accepted,
Of taking the Crown Jewels
Could be one of my final duels.
My heart is pounding in my chest,
Of stealing things I am the best.

Joshua Henderson (11)
Holy Ghost Catholic Primary School, Wandsworth

My Magic Pen

You think I'm writing this but that's not true.
I have a secret,
Between me and you.

I had a dream last night about a magic pen,
I tell it what to write and when.
It has great ideas,
It writes Christmas letters, poems and stories
And shopping lists for IKEA!

It looks just like a normal pen,
But it's in disguise.
It does cursive handwriting, the perfect size,
My poem might even win the *prize!*

David O'Connor (8)
Holy Ghost Catholic Primary School, Wandsworth

Amazing Candy Land

In my dreams every night I see a wonderful glistening place. People are so happy and nice like everyone is showing sweetness. One by one, they all give me some. When I look up the stars are dancing and twirling past me in the rainbow sky. Nature is beautiful because roses are red, violets are blue and candy is sweet and alive things too. Because now the dish ran away with the spoon.

Martina Formica (8)
Holy Ghost Catholic Primary School, Wandsworth

Missing Home

Buildings, bridges, all flickering with light
In the dead silence of the night,
The streets filled with closed stores,
Untouched by humans,
Parked empty machines everywhere.
Bridges, banks, homes, all crowded with citizens from all nations,
All kinds of shops and businesses fill the streets,
Cars and buses roaming everywhere,
This is Hong Kong.

Jenna Chu (11)
Holy Ghost Catholic Primary School, Wandsworth

Fantastic Unicorns

The first time I met my unicorn I was very shocked.
I found a hidden door in my bedroom and I nervously knocked...
I found myself in unicorn land, oh what a beautiful place!
Colourful, lovely unicorns in front of my face!
But one of them was special, she could make rainbows and fly.
She told me her name was Rainbow Sparkles and she took me to the sky!

Bianca Giuliari (7)
Holy Ghost Catholic Primary School, Wandsworth

Football Fever

It's football season once again!
Me, my friends and super FC Wimbledon.
I see a stadium with lots of seats, and the fans all stamp their feet!
I feel as excited as a crazy footballer on the pitch!
I score lots of goals as I make my fans twitch!
I win the match once again, as me and my team are the best!
And that is how my dream ends...

Alexander Broomfield (8)
Holy Ghost Catholic Primary School, Wandsworth

Monsters

M any of them come,

O n the night, sticking on your head like gum,

N one of them have smiley faces,

S abotaging our happy dreams they go in traces,

T alking to monsters is a nightmare,

E specially when you're in the night air,

R oughly every night I pray,

S o from now on I am safe!

Uma Santaolalla (7)

Holy Ghost Catholic Primary School, Wandsworth

Dreamland

You can do anything you want,
Run super fast,
You can jump super high,
Like you are on the moon.

In Dreamland, everyone is welcome,
There is no sadness, only endless joy.

In Dreamland, everyone is gentle,
No one is fighting.

In Dreamland, you can make candy houses,
A reward for your great behaviour.

Jean Carlos Orozco (8)
Holy Ghost Catholic Primary School, Wandsworth

The Lost Star

Out in space was a little star,
It was curious and wandered away far,
Out in space she was lost and alone,
She worried she was forever gone.
She cried and cried and made a puddle as big as a cloud.
Her tears began to light up as bright as the sun,
Her parents could see it from far,
This way they managed to find their lost star.

Cecilia Baiz Manthey (8)
Holy Ghost Catholic Primary School, Wandsworth

The Shadow Of The Night

I am the shadow,
The shadow of the night,
And up the wall, I take my flight,
From my eyes comes a light,
Your gate, it might be tight,
But your strength, I can fight.

I am the cat, the shadow of the night.

A hiss is my cry,
You think I fly,
Up to the sky,
Yes, I may die,
But I have nine lives.

Callum Graham (10)
Holy Ghost Catholic Primary School, Wandsworth

Magic Football

In my dream, clapping supporters cheer as loudly as an
erupting volcano,
Running quickly to score a golden goal,
Heading the ball like a kangaroo into the top corner,
Switching players, making the opponents dizzy,
Slide tackling swiftly when the referee isn't looking!
The final whistle blows and the battle is over!

Gonsague de Navacelle (8)
Holy Ghost Catholic Primary School, Wandsworth

Dancing

D ancing is the best as I take to the floor,

A nd all my nerves are shaking, like a terrified person,

N ow it is time for me to shine,

'C ause the light is on me!

E legantly as I dance something happens in my body, now I feel like I am floating across the stage, as I dance.

Katherine Brazdil (9)

Holy Ghost Catholic Primary School, Wandsworth

Ariel

With a wiggle, I am deeper than ever before.
Breathing in the absence of air is weird and wonderful.
A taste on my lips like ready salted crisps.
Surrounded by brilliant turquoise.
I miss my legs.
Neptune's call turns soft and motherly.
The dream slips from my mind like a fish from my hands.

Hannah Boffey (9)
Holy Ghost Catholic Primary School, Wandsworth

In My Dreams Every Night

In my dreams every night
I could be a knight
In my dreams every night
I would use all my might
In my dreams every night
I would be a hero and fight
The darkness of the night
Which gives my siblings a fright
In my dreams every night
Everything would be alright.

Balthazar Demortreux (7)
Holy Ghost Catholic Primary School, Wandsworth

Stage Fright

My eyes opened and a smile shone across my face. I spun enchantingly, my toes barely touching the ground. I leapt as gracefully as a gazelle, mouths hung open...
Suddenly, I collapsed, time stopped, I stood up and boos flew around the stage. I screamed and opened my eyes. What stage fright!

Éléonore de Navacelle (9)
Holy Ghost Catholic Primary School, Wandsworth

Dreams Of A Ballerina

B allet, ballet, lovely ballet,

A ssemblé, glissade, pas de chat,

L earning each new twist and turn,

L oving how my muscles burn,

E ach night I dream of Argentina,

T o dance as a famous ballerina!

Ilaria Delargy (8)

Holy Ghost Catholic Primary School, Wandsworth

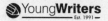

Dreams

As I disappeared into the land of candy, the clouds tasted like cotton candy. The fountains were filled with chocolate milk and the grass had rainbow candy stripes!
The sun was a giant yellow lollipop and the gingerbread people sang and danced in harmony.

Jannelle Chu (8)
Holy Ghost Catholic Primary School, Wandsworth

Swan Lake

A dancing fish sways against the indigo lake while fairies play tag. Lights start to ping along the soft mossy rocks as we hear *boom! Bang!* As the fireworks start the goblins go to bed. We hear the beautiful melody from the swans dancing on the lake.

Stella Burns (7)
Holy Ghost Catholic Primary School, Wandsworth

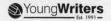

Dream

D uring the night, I become a footballer
R unning and dribbling around another player
E nabling my teammates to get the ball
A nd running until we score a goal
M aking us victorious once and for all.

Gregoire Cornet d'Elzius (9)
Holy Ghost Catholic Primary School, Wandsworth

Bats ~ Creatures Of The Night

Bats floating around in the night sky,
Their dark wings are flat and black.
Their squeals are louder than a cat's purr,
Rats above bats roam in the night,
Bats like gnats are unclean.

Jonah Nicola (8)
Holy Ghost Catholic Primary School, Wandsworth

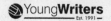

Flying Through The Sky

F lying through the sky,
L ike a bird so high,
Y ellow sun, shiny and warm,
I nspires me to glide,
N ear a golden eagle,
G uiding me back home.

Izzy Adam (8)
Holy Ghost Catholic Primary School, Wandsworth

The Trogglehumper

A haiku

A spine-chilling snarl,
A dark, inky black hallway,
The eeriest dream.

Ted Slater (9)
Holy Ghost Catholic Primary School, Wandsworth

The Blossom Tree

Here I am jumping out of the plane,
A moment ago, thinking I was mentally insane!
Now, I'm soaring through the marshmallow clouds,
While I'm hearing some wonderful sounds!
Then I spot an enormous tree,
Stretching further than I can see!
The tree is a lush blossom-pink,
But then I think, *I need a drink!*
Now I'm slowly drifting to the ground
Going down, down, down.
Then I land with a frown,
But then I find myself in my bed.
Then I realise, it is one of my lovely, lovely dreams...

Nye Taylor (8)
LIPA Primary School, Liverpool

The Wondrous World Of Dragons

As the day is about to end,
Up and up we ascend.
We soar across the open sky,
Further, we begin to fly.

Dragons! Big and small,
Some are short and some are tall.
Black and red and purple and green,
Some are calm and some are mean.

Above us a dragon that glows white,
She can brighten up the darkest night.
I'm riding on a dragon, coloured black,
At unexpected moments he attacks!

Olive Carey-Rios (10)
LIPA Primary School, Liverpool

Nightmare Land

Nightmare Land is full of dreads,
Makes children jump out of their beds.
Children scream, children run,
They don't know what's just begun.

Look out the window and you will see,
The scariest doll you ever did see.
They creep through the window and watch you in your sleep,
They don't stop haunting you until you're awake.
So pinch yourself for goodness sake.

Milah Waterfield (8)
LIPA Primary School, Liverpool

Untitled

I was going to the car,
But then I saw a big chocolate bar!
I got the chocolate bar and got in the car,
Then I drove very, very far!

I drove miles and miles,
Until I got to my stop,
I got out the car,
And heard a big plop!

I went to see
What the plop could be
But it was just a big bee
That had been squashed underneath me!

Rowan Hodgkinson-Hillan (7)
LIPA Primary School, Liverpool

Sweet Dreams

I was running, running running,
As fast as I could,
Hoping I would make it,
My head was pounding, pounding, pounding
I could barely breathe,
It was like I was being suffocated,
I was limping, limping,
Until...

I collapsed.

My head was banging, banging, banging
Where was I?

I managed to heave my eyes open,
I saw a blinding light above me,
My heart was beating, beating, beating,
The sound of silence screeched in my ear,
I was waiting, waiting, waiting,
I felt a clutch around my hand,
I sat up,
But nothing was on my hand, yet I could still feel it.

I looked around the room - it was all white!
Only white.
Was I still in solitary confinement?
Was I going insane?

Someone came in,
I hid under my covers,
Pretending I wasn't there,
They spoke: "I know you can hear me. I'm right here.
You will be okay."
Who were they?

I peeked through a hole in my covers,
A person dressed in all white,
An all-white tray,
With all-white food in their white-gloved hands,
Was that for me?
I felt a sharp pain stabbing my left hand as the clutch
on my other got tighter.

The mysterious person left,
I was exposed to the blinding light again,
I sat up,
But I couldn't,

I was trying, trying, trying,
I gave up,
My eyes shut immediately.

As the clutch on my hand got tighter than before,
It got tighter, tighter, tighter,
I finally caught my breath,
A scream left my mouth as a whisper,
My eyes opened slowly like the speed of a slug.

I saw what was clutching my hand:
My mum.
My dad was standing behind her, astonished,
I was breathing, breathing, breathing,
Only to realise there was a mask over my mouth.

I've been dreaming for weeks!

Zarah Gidman (11)
St John's CE Primary Academy, Stafford

The Columbia Rider

(Based on a true ride from Columbia.)

Once upon a time in Columbia, there was a very young boy called Alex and he loved riding the BMX, but there was a problem... there was only one bike for the whole family. Then something changed.

On his fifteenth birthday, he walked down the stairs to see his own bike. It was one of the best bikes in the world, but before his day could get any better, it did. He got a call from one of the best street riders in the world. He was offered the opportunity to fly out to New York and do a ride out with him and a load of other pro riders. So, he packed his stuff, grabbed his camera and hopped on a plane to New York.

As soon as he landed, there was a taxi waiting for him, so he got in. It took him to the villa where the pro riders were but it was late at night so he went to bed. The next day he got his phone out, made a YouTube account and started recording, but one rider wasn't happy with him recording so he pushed him off his bike and kept riding.

The next day, Alex posted the video and got loads of views. Now he is a pro rider who goes by the name Raazati.

Christian Till (11)
St John's CE Primary Academy, Stafford

From Dream To Hart To Proud; Will I Ever Escape?

Once upon a dream,
Unlike the world proud,
The houses float and loom,
Like a dreamy cloud.

The pathway is just like,
A rolled red carpet and,
Every step is just how Wand,
Made it to be.

All can be done there,
All except doing wrong
You feel like flying.
Do it for as long.

It's not all like this though,
There's another part.
Let's go to Hart.
It's different from this.

Welcome to Hart.
This will be your last,
Day of living your life,
Devils will come for your future and past.

The Hart might sound like a heart but,
Don't be deceived for this is just,
The opposite and a world of lust,
Whatever happens, never end up here for it will be your last.

There is a way back to life though,
Go through tunnel two,
To Proud - where you will never come back from or to,
For after 100 years, you will be a skeleton in your grave for eternity.

Bang! The doors of the tunnel were shut.
The only way is through,
Aargh! Penelope woke up to find the thing from her sleep,
The monster in Hart and all her nightmares threw.

The devil and its pet,
Every night she's awake.
Every time she sees that lake,
It all starts again.

This is none other than a nightmare,
One from the devil,
The dreams try to help her from the mares but,
Nothing could be done, for she's gone and was a rebel.

Ayomide Olaseinde (11)
St John's CE Primary Academy, Stafford

The Man On The Beach

One day, I woke up on the beach. It was dark and dusky on the beach. It was empty and all you could hear was the endless echo of seagulls squawking. In the distance, along the dull, musty sand, I saw a tall, dark-clothed man with a boat. I thought about escaping that awful place, so slowly I walked towards him. I started to run, desperate to leave but the more I ran, the more he started to fade.

Once I got to where he stood, there was nothing left of him. Just his boat. I quickly hopped in, not wanting to miss the opportunity to break free from this wet place. I started to row into the still, dark sea but not long after, something from in the water grabbed my arm and pulled me into the cold, deep sea. It all went dark. I woke up back on the beach, lying on the sand, as dry as a bone, like nothing happened. On my arm was a scar from where I was grabbed. I stood up and saw a tall, dark-clothed man with a boat...

Abigail Hillis (11)
St John's CE Primary Academy, Stafford

The Altered Paradise

I awakened feeling faint,
Trying to take in my surroundings,
The sky was a diamond glistening blue,
Whilst the sun teased me with its sharp stinging rays.

Bubbles floated past me,
Like hot-air balloons dancing in the sky.
The grass was an emerald-green,
That tickled my feet as I brushed by,
But something didn't feel right.

The walls were closing in,
The room was getting smaller,
And smaller,
And smaller.

I was startled by a deafening noise that pierced my
ears.
Screech!
It got louder and louder.
I clenched my ears for dear life until,
I gave up.

Alas I woke up,
With my ears ringing,
My head banging,
And my body shaking.
I looked around me.
I was in the same room,
Except everything was altered.

The sky was a midnight-blue,
And the sun was a dark gold.
It didn't have that warm feeling anymore,
It was just pale.
The grass was dead and stiff,

And the bubbles fell weakly to the ground.
The clouds were grey and heavy,
And alas, it was raining.

Chioma Anyanwu (11)
St John's CE Primary Academy, Stafford

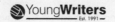

The Creature In My Dreams

As I woke up, I felt like I was in a different house,
The wall was crooked and the lights were dim and slowly dying,
I had never felt this before, normally I felt safe,
But I felt like I was being watched, it felt like a nightmare.

I got out of bed and got hit by uneasy air,
I opened the door to see an unreal hallway,
I wanted to go back but the door disappeared,
I hit the wall with a thwack, thwack, but it wouldn't break.

I heard a noise come from my left,
As I looked towards it I saw a weird, broken and glitchy person!
Lanky arms started to come out and it ripped itself, to show a tall scary creature,
It ran as fast as a cheetah, nearly giving me no chance to run.

As I ran it got faster and faster until it nearly got me,
But I got tripped by it and it started to pull me,
I hit it as hard as I could but it wouldn't budge,
As I accepted my fate, I shot up out of my bed and looked around,

I figured out it was just a dream, a bad dream,
But on my legs were strange handprints, so I thought,
was it really a dream?

Lucas Rogers (11)

St John's CE Primary Academy, Stafford

The Flick Of A Flame

The strong wind blasting me off my feet,
Three days of torture still begging for something to eat.
I need aid, or maybe just a place to stay out of this
maze.
But little did I know it was just a haze.

I saw a flame, so bright,
And it danced through the whole night.
Then all of a sudden I jumped up, a new winter day.
It must've been a dream - hooray!

Then I saw the flame again, but small,
And dancing, but wanting to be tall.
As I went to the field to see the flicker of the flame,
I ran over and surprisingly it was tame.

The wind blew strong then - there was no light,
It was all a big fright.
This fire had gone out.
I wished a match would come about.

My vision getting dimmer and dimmer,
The thought of a fire getting slimmer and slimmer.
Until there was a star,
But sadly it was too far.

Whoosh! Then there was light,
And the fires again danced through the night.
In the morning without a doubt,
The fire had gone out.

Jordon Phelps (11)
St John's CE Primary Academy, Stafford

The Stalker

As I started walking,
It hit me,
Although I couldn't see it,
I could still hear it,
That's when I knew something or someone was
following me,
I turned around to see,
A strange creature following me,
How long had this been following me,
It may have been forever but I would never know,
The story behind,
It may be strange, so I didn't want to hear it,
I slowly began to run,
As it came after me,
There was no turning back now,
I stumbled upon an old ragged cottage in the woods,
I ran inside to hide from the creature,
Later that day it found the cottage,
I ran to a room to hide,
That's when I heard a noise,
Bang!
"What was that noise?"
"Was it the creature?"

The door began to open,
I began to scream,
"Is this a dream?"
But all of a sudden,
I woke up,
Maybe it was just a dream,
Or was it...?

Iyla-Mai Crossley (11)
St John's CE Primary Academy, Stafford

Asylum

I felt lost
I sensed I was not alone,
Not the only one roaming this empty path.
I was grabbed,
Argh!

I opened my eyes,
A world of white,
My mind filled with whats and whys,
Though I knew I was grabbed at night.

I sat there petrified,
Not knowing left or right, up or down,
I tried to move my arms, I couldn't,
I was in an asylum,
I had to let that sink in!

My dreams were crushed that night,
Vanished out of sight.
I went to sleep,
Ready to weep.

There was a sombre knock at the door,
A figure in a cloak, a dark black one is what they wore,
Untied me,
I realised I was free.

Fifty years I sat there
Fifty years alone,
No dream to hold onto,
No place to call home.

Now I sit here thinking,
About what I did wrong,
What made them crush my dreams,
But they could still have their own.

Nancy Bull (11)

St John's CE Primary Academy, Stafford

The Dream Of The World

Once upon a world called a dream,
The cobblestone pathways twist and turn and the brick
walls are as smooth as a thin sheet of plastic.
The red brick walls are so red, the shine of it could
blind someone,
As you walk you can see the action, its waves,
And the clouds are so soft they are like cotton candy.

If you go into a building, it would feel like it is levitating
As if someone is controlling it.
You can never hear any loud noises because it is a
peaceful city.
Every step is a caution.

The air in the city is like a gas that fills you up with joy.
It is a wonderful city each time the sun comes up, it is
smiling.
The sun is full of happiness.
But, the moon is full of sadness.

And the light shines through night and day.
And the lampposts are as stiff as can possibly be.
And the light in the water can show life.

Fraser Parsons (11)
St John's CE Primary Academy, Stafford

The Mysterious Dream

In a dream, there was a jungle,
It stood tall and proud,
The animals used the jungle as a home,
There was an old, abandoned hospital.

No animal went in the hospital,
One animal went in once and never came out,
They blocked the entrance to the hospital,
No one could get in.

One night, some lights in the hospital turned on,
The owls flew up to have a look,
there was a human-like figure,
When it saw the owls, it disappeared.

They flew back down and warned everyone,
They sent a group of animals to look for the figure,
When they were deep into the hospital, there was no
sign of it,
They found a room full of supplies.

They found the creature,
It had animal bones in the room,
They were scared and ran away,
They were so scared, they ran away forever.

Ernie Kenderdine (11)
St John's CE Primary Academy, Stafford

Inside A Hole!

On my way to school,
I tumbled into a hole,
It was a big black hole,
Inside the hole was a long, dark corridor,
Inside the long, dark corridor,
There was a long purple line,
Above the long purple line read,
'Follow me if you dare',
At the end of the long purple line was an eye,
On top of that eye was a small panda,
I greeted the small panda,
He showed me a golden path,
At the end of the golden path,
There was a rat; I followed the rat to a gap,
On the other side of the gap,
There was me! All cosy asleep!
I must be dreaming,
What a creepy dream,
I woke up and looked at my clock,
It was nearly seven o'clock,
I turned over and saw a rat!
Fast asleep in my hamster's cage!

So, was it a dream?
Or was it real?
Nobody knows!

Iyla Rose Copestake (10)
St John's CE Primary Academy, Stafford

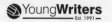
Welcome To My World

Welcome to Dreamland, I'll give you a tour
I'll take you around like a private chauffeur
Here in my dream, everything is as I choose
My dream is my world I cannot lose.

Here is my world the rivers flow with juice
Beds made of oranges where people snooze
The skies as blue as a diamond
With roaring cotton candy clouds behind them.

Streets made of chocolate bars
People playing football with Mars
As crazy and weird as this may seem
I can assure you this is just a dream.

We're nearly done, just a bit more
With wide open toffee doors
Animals run wild and free
Next to the emerald-green sea.

Time to wake up, goodbye dream
It's time to go, time to leave
My dream world is gone, back in the past
Back to reality at last.

Devansh Pun (11)
St John's CE Primary Academy, Stafford

The Aurora Borealis

It was dark, I awoke from my slumber,
What was that? That beautiful, enticing light,
Could it really be true?
My, oh my! That beautiful, enticing sight!

Then I was dumbstruck,
My one and only wish,
Just my luck,
The one and only *Aurora Borealis!*

The Aurora Borealis dances in the sky,
I feel funny, I suddenly whirl,
I kick and I scream, why, oh why?
I'm back in my room, and with delight, I twirl.

I follow my dream with courage,
You'll follow yours, too!
For I can't keep more dreams in storage,
They too must be pursued!

My dreams had come true,
So why not yours too?
I'll let it take as long as it needs,
But I'm forever determined to pursue my dreams!

Ore-Ofe Taiwo (10)
St John's CE Primary Academy, Stafford

Disco Nightmare

The dancefloor pulls you in,
The bar sells a lot of gin,
Lily is the best,
But then she got sent on a quest.

A mystery envelope showed up at her feet,
The writing was very neat,
She sensed someone watching her,
Then she heard a brrr.

She followed it onto the dance floor,
Suddenly she fell against the door,
Everything went black,
She woke up in a sack.

Her heart was beating so fast,
All the dancing was in the past,
Who knows what Lily was supposed to do,
Everything went blue.

Lily heard a familiar sound,
Beep, beep the sound fell to the ground,
It was her alarm clock,
Her mum was at the door ready to knock.

Lily's dream job used to be a dancer,
Not anymore after this disaster.

Phoebe Bull (11)
St John's CE Primary Academy, Stafford

The Tunnel That Sees

Dark, damp, dread, the flame
Went out, and I hear
Them, the eyes laughing
And dancing and mocking me,
My own head echos in the
Tunnels, I hear the silence
Buzzing in my ears

I long for an exit on the way
I hear my own echoes, my own
Thoughts, as I only hear
Drip,
Drip,
Drip,
It makes me go mad
I run and run and run and run
But it sees me
The tunnel won't stop tormenting me

I feel like I've
Fallen in a pit of my
Own self-pity consuming
All my hope of leaving here
Will I wake, will I see light?

Will I go insane before I get
Lost in my own mindscape
I feel completely lost
But I wake up
And I then see
It's just a dream inside the tunnel's eyes.

Lucas Brewis (11)
St John's CE Primary Academy, Stafford

Life In Dreamland

In the dreamland that I met
The floor was covered in clouds
There were little birds that were singing
The most lovely songs that I had ever heard

The bushes were made of cotton candy
And the path was made of sweets
Suddenly, I felt my mouth watering
Wanting to eat them all
The chocolate bunnies hopped on the fluffy pink clouds
They were so cute that I wanted to pet them all

And the sun was so bright that it blinded my eyes
And the sky was so blue
That it looked like diamonds
Then I saw a girl show up in a shop
Selling scrumptious desserts that were as cold as snow

Up in the dreamland
Where everything was nice
It was the most dreamy place
That I had ever dreamed.

Himanthi Samaranayake (11)
St John's CE Primary Academy, Stafford

The Watcher

I feel someone watching me,
They get closer every second,
I turn around and see nothing,
I run as fast as I can,
They match my pace as I run.

They are in front of me with glowing red eyes,
Their twisted grin gives me the chills,
They move closer and closer,
I stand there frozen like a statue,
Then *bang!* I'm in a damp tunnel with them.

They stare at me with a grin,
I try to run, but they are too strong; I look down,
And see they have a knife...

They drop me on the ground,
They just stand there, laughing at me,
They turn into a human, and I become The Watcher.

Now it's my turn to watch,
I stalk the street I died on,
Waiting for my victim.

Megan Barron (11)
St John's CE Primary Academy, Stafford

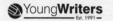

Don't Take The Wrong Turn

Everything is the same,
I'm fed up,
But not today,
Today was different,
In the worst possible way,

It started in the sun,
And then in the maze,
By taking the wrong turn,
I am now in the grave,
With a cold bone,
And no home,

Everything is the same,
But it's not,
Why is it raining?
Why is it burning?
Oh no, it's acid,

It started in the sun,
But now in the rain,
With burning skin,
I start to struggle,
I try and walk,
But instead I hobble,

Everything is the same,
But I'm bleeding away,
What was the point of my seven years of living,
Just to bleed away, now everything is different.

Iyla-Rose Walters-Clark (11)
St John's CE Primary Academy, Stafford

The Space Alien

I got ready for this nervous trip,
Ready to board the scared ship,
I got my signal to look out,
But then I got knocked out.

Then I jumped up in surprise,
I looked around to find my prize,
But then I found a thing,
Who was not usual at all.

Bang! It disappeared in thin air,
Now I was getting very confused,
Who was this thing and where did it come from?
This mystery was a weird one.

I walked along the hallway waiting for a signal,
Waiting for someone to lure me through,
I tried to open the large door,
The door felt like it was stuck like glue.

Then I woke up. It was all a dream.

Alona Shinu (11)
St John's CE Primary Academy, Stafford

Life In Dreamland

In Dreamland, the ground was covered in clouds,
And the birds chirped at me.
The pretty flowers would hang on the stars,
Up in the sky.
The bushes were made of sweets,
And the path was made of chocolate.

The children hopped on the soft white clouds,
And the sky was jet-black.
The floating shops were filled with delicious desserts,
When it was day, the sun was so bright, it blinded my
eyes.
Then I saw a girl show up in a shop,
Selling scrumptious desserts that were as cold as snow.

Up in Dreamland,
Where everything was nice.
It was the most dreamy place,
That I've ever seen.

Anusha Gurung (11)
St John's CE Primary Academy, Stafford

A Christmas Dream

In this world, there is nothing to fear,
Your dreams are here.
In this place, you can believe,
Now we must start celebrating for Christmas Eve.
Just let the lights wink, wink, wink,
In every colour that you can think.
Wishes may be granted,
But never as an advantage.
Always remember to leave Santa some candy,
It could come in handy.
Santa helps the reindeer to land,
Even though the elves need to give them a hand.
Now, a basic tree becomes full of joy,
Because under it lies a toy.
That is the end of my fabulous dream,
So now I must awaken before Christmas morning has
been.

Sarah Wright (11)
St John's CE Primary Academy, Stafford

Christmas Eve

The dream world starts here,
There is nothing to fear.
Everything you believe shall be achieved,
Now let's start celebrating for Christmas Eve.
Dull sky becomes brighter than you think,
Let the bright, colourful lights wink.
A gift may be granted,
But never as an advantage.
Don't forget to give Santa some candy,
It will probably come in handy.
The reindeer will land,
The elves will give Santa a hand.
When you finally go to sleep,
He will come and sneak.
A basic tree becomes something like you have never seen,
Now that is the end of my fabulous dream.

Zoe Parsons (11)
St John's CE Primary Academy, Stafford

Creative Spirit

Once upon a dream, a young boy believed,
Once upon a dream, a boy became a thief,
Soon the time will come when another dream will form,
He'll leave it in the past, that's why they never last,
They'll be left behind, somewhere you can't find.

These dreams are very powerful, powerful indeed,
Enter your creative spirit, then you'll see,
The power of dreams is more powerful than you can
see.

So everything you dream, you'd better believe,
Follow your dreams, try and believe.

Enter your creative spirit and finally, you'll see.

Baptiste Feliste (11)
St John's CE Primary Academy, Stafford

Oh World!

Oh, world!
Oh, trees
Oh, all the things you bring.

Like the dazzling stars and moonlit sky!
Oh, if I could fly like a bird, in the blue blue sky!
Oh, if I could swim like a fish, in the deep sea,
But if I could stop climate change,
I would work in every way,
Work harder for the polar bears,
Harder for the bees,
Harder for our wonderful world!

Oh, if the world was right,
Then everything would thrive,
We could save the polar bears, birds and bees if they
were fluttering in the sky!

Oh, what wonders you bring,
Oh, world!

Isabelle Pasquill (11)
St John's CE Primary Academy, Stafford

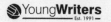

The Vampire's True Death

As I crept into the room,
There she lay,
As fierce as a tiger,
I crept closer,
But she slowly faded away,
I fled as fast as a bullet,
I despise you, Penelope,
I will turn you,
Now I must wait.

She's awoken,
I must leave her?
You will get what you deserve,
You will feel the consequences,
Here we go,
Wait what, how are you awake?
Wait, no.

People were crowding me I felt a sharp pain,
It was like a thousand daggers digging into my skin,
I fell to the ground in pain.

Theo Middleton (11)
St John's CE Primary Academy, Stafford

YouTube

Once upon a dreamland,
YouTube was the best platform.
In a dreamland,
I was the smallest channel.

Around the corner,
Let's not forget,
How much the views sky-rocketed,
Increasing by the second, I think I need some venom.

Let's not forget,
How high they can get.
How many views, I don't hear a steam,
Wait, wait, what if this was a dream too?

Never bet, I just don't see, why would it be?
I wake up. Why did it have to be a dream?

Noah Wrotchord (10)
St John's CE Primary Academy, Stafford

The Night Terror

As I was asleep
I was awoken with a scare
The devil in my room
With his haunting glare.

I cried in fright
And he wanted a fight
He wanted me to go to Hell
But I shouted for help.

He looked around my room and took my bear
Then I choked on the air
The devil ripped the head off
Fluff went everywhere.

I screamed for my mum
No matter how much I screamed, nobody came
Somehow, I dozed back to sleep
And awoke with no devil in my view.

Skyla Adams (10)
St John's CE Primary Academy, Stafford

The Dream Experience

One day as I fell asleep
In a big dream deep
As my imagination flees,
Inside a world of wonder,

I wake up in my dream,
It was strange as I could see,
A snowy forest with a path,
With no seat,

A wonder went mind,
A path as a dime,
Trembling I go,
Upon a cottage I see,
As I walk upon the door,
Knock, knock I go,

No one was home,
Therefore I was alone,
A dancing fire to my side,
After a time I was dreaming so.

Ethan Harley (11)
St John's CE Primary Academy, Stafford

The Shadow

It's upside down in Dreamland,
Where nothing is bland.
There's always white snow
And you even get to row.

Everyone was underwater with their snorkel
Until everyone saw a mysterious portal.
It was centred
So everyone entered.

It all went dark...
Whoosh! Through came a shadow.
It was all silent.
Bang! The gunshot was as loud as a bomb.

The shadow was gone.
It was all back to normal
But it still felt... wrong!

I woke up,
Surely with some luck.
It was a bad dream,
I was very relieved.

Daniel Ross (11)
St John's CE Primary Academy, Stafford

My Dream Life

When I was young, I wanted
To be a vet when I was older,
I love animals
But not spiders sadly.

Happily, I would say to Mum and Dad,
I wanted to be a vet when I am older
I jumped in surprise when I got the job,
I would burst like a balloon
So happy that I felt like a
Happy, smiley sun.

I was helping the vet,
On my first day, I made
So many friends.
But then I woke up.
It was all a dream.

Ellie Booth (11)
St John's CE Primary Academy, Stafford

My Journey With The Wizard

In my dreams, every night, this wizard comes to take me up, up, up, and away. I am not ready, and I am not sure, but, in the end, she takes me to a dinosaur! It roars and bellows, stomps and screeches but soon it orders, "Will you give me that piece of meat?"
I pick up the red, juicy meat for the scary, enormous dinosaur to chomp and eat.
From top to bottom, I see his tail wiggling endlessly from the trail. His eyes are gleaming like a star while his arms cannot reach so far. I can see that he will pass away very soon so to cheer him up, I give him a big, green dinosaur balloon.
"Oh, thank you very much. You are a nice girl, I am so happy I could twirl," says the dinosaur.
Soon, the wizard announces, "Come on, say your goodbyes and farewell!"
Because we are in a hurry, we shoot into the blue, midnight sky, so fast we are blurry. Then, we make it to the royal castle, where we see a princess hassled by a bee.
"What's wrong?" I ask.
"Well, we don't have a song, and if we don't have a song, it could all go wrong!" screams the princess.
"Just use your mind and see what you find!"

Then, we go up, up, up, until we make it into space with a calm grace. To our surprise, we find an astronaut trying to put tea in a teapot. The milk he's using for his tea, came from the space cow tree. He is sipping slowly as a tortoise.

"That's one step for tea, and one giant gulp for me!"

In the end, she takes me to my house, back for bedtime with my toy mouse.

Aisosa Lucky-Sunday (9)
Woodhouse Primary Academy, Quinton

My Nightmare Monster

M y monster only appears at night, it is
Y ellow with green spots and purple warts, it smells like

N asty mould and rotting fish
I n my dreams it eats fairies and unicorns
G rinding its teeth that look like swords
H appy thoughts turn grim around it but a
T eam once did defeat it but it
M agically returned so we raise our spears
A nd go into battle. Who will win? Nobody knows
R iot is all that can be seen or heard
E ventually, we stab our spear right into his heart

M oans, groans can be heard as he shrinks into a kitten
O w goes Grumpt (who has been hit by forever grumpiness)
N estled down beside her, nursing her leg
S ilently, everyone looks around in an old graveyard,
T iny mews from the least scary monster
E rased from my memory as soon as I wake up
R epeating every night, forever and ever, in my head at night.

Violet Stevens (9)
Woodhouse Primary Academy, Quinton

How Life Is...

Beautiful sunny day
I wonder how life is
Shimmering around my eyes
What a damp sun
How will it be?
I wonder, I wonder
I wonder how poor people survive
With their tiny cardboard
And torn clothes
I wonder how rich people live
In their big mansions
Big room
Everything is huge
I wonder how animals live
Eating their prey
Dying each day
Thank god I'm not an animal
There are a lot of things to know on this Earth
Each day and night, something happens and nobody
knows
Perhaps I will know soon...

Toba Okunaiya (9)
Woodhouse Primary Academy, Quinton

My Famous Wish

I wish I was famous like Taylor Swift, flying high like a
kite in the sky,
Singing sweet songs that make people sigh.
Or writing great stories like books on a shelf,
Inspirational like Chimamanda herself.
Or playing my guitar with tunes high and low,
Like Ed Sheeran's music, making hearts glow.
Or ruling the stage, with a voice loud and clear,
With Beyoncé's voice, spreading joy far and near.
Or dancing enthusiastically brightening the sky
extremely bright,
With hits like Dua Lipa illuminating the night.

Tammy Alao (9)
Woodhouse Primary Academy, Quinton

The Little Dragon

My dreams have taken me out of this land,
There I see a little furious black dragon,
Holding an arrow of fire in its left hand.
It looks scary, like a demon.
Wishing now to have a closer look.
As I move towards the animal,
It feels wonderful and magical,
Just like in my favourite storybook.
But the little dragon tries to attack me,
I immediately run and hide behind a tree,
Before waking up,
And then realised I was having a nap.

Mathieu Nkengni (9)
Woodhouse Primary Academy, Quinton

My Love Of Maths

In my dreams every night maths is red and also bright.
I am very good at maths and I cannot wait for my
SATs.

I love times tables because they are fun to do.
I love algebra too.

My school motto is 'achieve, inspire, believe and
dream'.
I shine as light, as light as a beam.

Courtney Francis (9)
Woodhouse Primary Academy, Quinton

YOUNG WRITERS INFORMATION

We hope you have enjoyed reading this book – and that you will continue to in the coming years.

If you're a young writer who enjoys reading and creative writing, or the parent of an enthusiastic poet or story writer, do visit our website **www.youngwriters.co.uk**. Here you will find free competitions, workshops and games, as well as recommended reads, a poetry glossary and our blog.

If you would like to order further copies of this book, or any of our other titles, then please give us a call or visit **www.youngwriters.co.uk**.

Young Writers
Remus House
Coltsfoot Drive
Peterborough
PE2 9BF
(01733) 890066
info@youngwriters.co.uk

 YoungWritersUK YoungWritersCW
 youngwriterscw youngwriterscw